Black, Beautiful, and Creatively Empowered

BERNETTA WATSON

authorHOUSE®

AuthorHouse™
1663 Liberty Drive
Bloomington, IN 47403
www.authorhouse.com
Phone: 1 (800) 839-8640

Published by AuthorHouse 06/08/2017

ISBN: 978-1-5246-9489-0 (sc)
ISBN: 978-1-5246-9488-3 (e)

Table of Contents

Black Beautiful And Creatively Empowered

A book for African American adolescent girls ages 10-18 years old. Read information about the stages of adolescence, self-esteem, self-confidence, setting goals and being a leader.

Bernetta "Breezy" Watson

Introduction

Girls you are changing from childhood into adolescence.

Many changes will occur in your life. Your body will began to change, there will be physical changes, like your breast will began to develop, menstruation can start you will began puberty (the period in which the human body becomes capable of reproduction). You will go through social, emotional and cognitive (thinking and making decisions about the right things to do and say).

When I think about a beautiful butterfly it remains me of the changes adolescent girls go through. The butterfly goes through a metamorphosis this is the magic that insects teach us that change ensures growth.

"Quote" Maya Angelou

"We delight in the beauty of the butterfly but rarely realize the changes it has gone through to achieve that beauty."

The meaning of adolescent

An adolescent is a young person in the process of developing from a child into an adult.

The period between puberty and adulthood.

3 staged of adolescence by age.

Early age 11-14

Middle age 15-17

Late 18-21

The stages of adolescence is puberty, physical development, intellectual

Development, emotional development, social development.

Puberty is the process of physical changes through which a child's body matures into an adult.

Physical development is the process that starts in human infancy and continues into late adolescents concentrating on gross and fine motor skills as well as puberty.

Intellectual development is the measure of how individual learn to think and reason for themselves in the world around them.

Emotional development refers to a child's growing ability to regulate and control emotions and form secure relationships.

Social development involves learning values, knowledge and skills that enable children to relate to others effectively.

Positive Self-Esteem

Positive self-esteem gives you the strength and flexibility and confidence to take charge of your life and grow from your mistakes without the fear of rejection.

1. Say positive things about yourself.

2. Learn to accept compliments, just say thank you when someone says something nice about you to you.

3. Let go the need to always be right or perfect.

4. Know that mistakes are learning opportunities not failures.

5. Negative thinking about yourself can lower your self-esteem

6. Maintaining your personal hygiene and personal appearance can improve your self-esteem.

7. Always make sure that you bath daily, use deodorant change undergarments daily, more if needed.

8. Brush your teeth and use mouth wash to prevent bad breath.

9. Be well groomed, wear clean and pressed clothes and clean shoes and socks.

10. Make sure your nails and hands are clean, nails are filed, no chipped nail polish. Use lotion on your hands to keep them soft and looking healthy.

11. The items that you need for good hygiene and grooming can be purchased for a reasonable cost at a dollar store or a popular pharmacy in your neighborhood.

The meaning of self-esteem and self-confidence and the difference

Self-esteem is internal it means accepting and appreciating yourself for who you are.

Self-confidence is external it is to do the things you fear and get success is how you feel about your abilities.

You can have healthy self-esteem but low self-confidence.

When you love yourself, your self-esteem improves which makes you more confident.

Social Skills

Social skills are used to interact and communicate with others using verbal and nonverbal ways. The process of learning these skills is socialization. It is very important to develop good social skills.

Social skills are ways of dealing with others that create a healthy and positive interaction.

Social skills are just getting along with others. Your social skills start when you are very young, you learn to play with other children and you learn good behavior and sharing.

A person's social skills can be based on their, language, where they grow up and the number of children in the family. No matter what our situation is we must learn good social skills to be comfortable in our interaction with others at home, school, work or any social setting.

Life Skills

Life skills are used in everyday life. Any skill that is useful in your life can be a life skill. Personal skills are the most important skills you need, bathing, getting dressed, brushing your teeth, combing hair, these skills are needed to maintain a healthy body and mind.

One life skill that is very important is the ability to use positive behavior like knowing how to get along with others.

To list a very few life skills that are as simple as tying your shoe laces, cleaning your bed room, swimming, driving a car, using a computer, going to school or work and cooking. Any skill that is useful in your life can be considered a life skill.

Civility Skills

Civility is polite acts or expressions of respectful behavior. Just speaking saying hello to someone is an act of a civility skill. Saying thank you is a good civility skill or allowing someone to enter the door before you or helping an elderly lady or man with their grocery bags.

Civility is the act of being kind to others.

Civility Skills

Being civil is being kind to others, doing random acts of kindness.

Always be kind, polite and courteous to others.

Society needs more people with good civility skills.

Poem by Bernetta Watson

Quote: Maya Angelo

"I've learned that people will forget what you said, people will forget what you did, but people will never forget how you made them feel." Maya Angelo

Negative Gestures

Refrain from negative gestures. These are things you can do that make others feel uncomfortable not showing good manners or respect for others.

Don't cough or sneeze without covering your mouth, use a tissue or handkerchief, wash your hands or use hand sanitizer.

Don't point or stare at people it make them feel uncomfortable; the person could think you are saying something about them that is hurtful.

Don't whisper to a person in front of others, that is rude behavior and makes others feel bad.

Don't chew gum, making smacking sounds, pulling the gum out of your mouth or blowing bubbles in public.

Don't interrupt when someone is talking learn to be a good listener.

Remember to prevent negative gestures you must be thoughtful, kind, respectful, treat others with consideration. Rudeness is offensive behavior, impolite and makes others feel hurt.

Be Respectful To Adults

Please be respectful to adults never speak in a rude way to an adult.

Always put a Miss, Mr., or Mrs. in front of an adult's name.

Never use slang talk with an adult when answering a question.

Please do not shake your head, say yes or no or yes Ma'am, yes Sir or no Sir.

As a young person if you have a problem with an adult talk to your parents to help solve your issues. Do no talk back to an adult.

Communication Skills

1. Listening is a skill that is important, listening is the foundation of communication you can make better decisions when you listen.

2. Verbal is talking is a way of communicating with words.

3. Signs and symbols, there are signs and symbols everywhere, some popular signs are stop signs, yield right of way signs, school signs, hospital, street crossing signs, and traffic lights. When we see these signs we know what they mean. When we see the golden arches we know it is McDonalds. When we see the USA flag on a pole in the air we know that is a symbol of freedom, justice, pride and respect. We know our flag is red, white and blue and each color has a meaning.

4. Television is a form of communication we get news and find out what is going on in the world.

5. Telephone is a form of communication a fast way of getting in touch with a person local or long distance; this is a way of having a verbal conversation.

6. Computer is an electronic device for storing and processing data and is able to store a program and retrieve information from its memory. It is a rapid form of communication.

7. Writing is putting words on paper or composing a text, words that are coherent and understandable. A thank-you-note should always be hand written, you should always write a thank-you-note when someone give you a gift or treat you to a dinner or a day out at an event.

8. Body language is more effective at times than words, 95% communication is body language. Facial expression, the way we hold our head, stand, movement of our body.

9. Interpersonal communication skills are the skills that we use when we engaged in face-to-face communication with one or more persons.

Body Language

Body language is one of the most important

Forms of communication it is nonverbal.

Body language speaks loudly.

Body movement facial expressions, eye movement, gesture that you make, posture can express how you feel without saying a word.

Body language can let people know who you are and your mood and attitude.

Dr. Albert Mehrabian, author of Silent Messages conducted several studies on nonverbal communication. He found that 7% of any message is conveyed through words, 38% through certain vocal elements, and 55% through nonverbal (facial expression, gestures, posture, etc.)

Making An Introduction

Always make sure you introduce people that you know are meeting for the first time.

Introductions should be made as follows:

A young person to and older person

A man to a woman

A young person to your parents

A boy to a girl

Introduce your mother or father to your friend's mother or father.

When in school, you should introduce your parents to your school principal or teacher. Always include the last name when making introductions except when introducing members of your family whose last names are the same as yours.

If your parents name differs from yours give their last name.

Example:

Introducing a younger person to an older person:

Jiamond this is my grandmother Mrs. Anna Bell Blackwell. Grandmother this is my friend from school Jiamond

Introducing your parents to your teacher:

Mom and dad, this is my teacher Ms. Troublefield. Ms. Troublefield, these are my parents Celia and Thomas Wainwright.

When you introduce people always give some background information about the person, nothing personal.

Example:

Alice this is Brenda my friend that makes the floral arrangements that I told you about.

Handshake

This custom started in medieval times (British) it lasted 5th to the 15th century people often concealed weapons in their hands. The handshake was of affirming that neither you nor the person you were greeting was caring anything intended to harm, over time it evolved into a polite greeting.

The way we greet people in the United State is with a handshake and pleasant verbal greeting, like hello, nice to meet you or it is good to see you.

When Chinese meet they may bow or nod slightly. In some cultures like India the men only shake hands with men.

Handshake

1. First stand up

2. Make eye contact

3. Smile

4. Say something pleasant, give a verbal greeting like it nice to see you, hello how are you? it is good to see you, I have been looking forward to meeting you.

5. Extend the right hand with the thumb up and fingers together. Give firm handshake 2 or 3 pumps (the hand moving in an up and down movement or motion.)

6. Don't give a weak or limp noodle handshake it gives a bad impression that you don't have character or not interested in meeting the person.

7. A strong handshake could mean confidence.

These are some occasions you give a handshake:

1. Meeting someone for the first time.

2. When you give greetings to a person you know.

3. When saying goodbye.

4. When you receive an award or give one.

5. When congratulating someone on a special achievement.

6. When you are closing a business deal.

7. Before and after a job interview.

8. When meeting your friend's parents for the first time.

The Meaning Of Good Manners

Good manners are the treatment of other people with courtesy and politeness and showing correct public behavior and at home.

Good manners are acting in a way that is socially acceptable and respectful with consideration for others.

Good manners are doing unto others as you would have them do unto you.

Saying thank you, please, you are welcome, excuse me, and good morning with a smile are words used when we practice good manners. Always speak when you enter a room.

MANNERS DON'TS

1. Do not gossip

2. Do not disrespect your family and friends.

3. Do not chew gum making popping sounds, don't pull your gum out of your mouth in public it is rude.

4. Do not touch people or stand to close without their permission.

5. Do not touch other people's belongings without their permission.

6. Do not lie

7. Do not talk about your family's personal business without your parent's permission.

8. Do not be late for school and other appointments.

9. Do not use profanity or unpleasant words.

10. Do not be rude do not talk when someone else is talking be a good listener.

11. Do not talk back to your parents and other adults.

12. Do not make fun others clothing or shoes.

Good Manners

Good manners last a life time.

Good manners will open doors for you.

Good manners will get you invited to social events.

Good manners will allow your friends to enjoy being around you.

Good manners is saying please, thank you, excuse me, good morning and you are welcome.

GOOD MANNERS WILL LAST A LIFE TIME.

Poem by Bernetta Watson

Proper Etiquette

The meaning of etiquette is a (ticket) is a French word. When the French Royals attended a celebration they were given a ticket (etiquette) that told them were to stand and not to stand on the grass at Royal celebration.

Etiquette is a code of polite conduct, good behavior, rules and codes, customs and courtesy you are less likely to offend or annoy people if you practice proper etiquette.

SOME ETIQUETTE RULES

1. RSVP is a French phrase Respond if you please. When you receive an invitation that says RSVP by a certain date, the person that is planning the affair needs to know the number of guest for food and drinks, preparation, space and seating.

2. Knowing which fork to use when eating a meal, start with the outside and work inward in using your eating utensils.

3. When you receive a gift of any kind you should write a thank-you-note. Thank you notes are always hand written.

4. Handshakes, there is a correct way to shake hands in the USA.

5. No brushing or flossing your teeth in public, no brushing or combing your hair in public. No clipping or filing your nails in public, do not put on your lipstick at the table after a meal.

6. Do not use your cell phone in public lines or public places like, the post office, grocery store, department of motor vehicle, restaurants, movies theaters, and no texting while driving a car.

Faux Pas

The word faux pas comes from the French and means (False step). It is a noun and is pronounced fo pa.

A faux pas is an embarrassing or tactless act or remark in a social situation, a word or behavior that is a social mistake.

EXAMPLE: you are with a group of people and you start to talk about a person but you did not know it was a close family member of one of the people in the group and it hurt and embarrassed the person because other people were aware of the family connection.

EXAMPLE: you were talking about a friend you did not know she was standing near and could hear you talking about her.

When you commit a faux pas apologize and keep it moving, don't make a big scene and do not continue to discuss the mistake.

Posture

Posture is a part of your body image as well as proper fitting clothing.

Be sure you sit straight in a chair, legs crossed at the ankles

Do not slump when you sit because it can give the idea that you do not feel good about yourself or just lazy

When you sit in a chair do it smoothly, be elegant, and sit easy

Let the back of your knees touch the chair, lower yourself, keep your body straight, sit down, slide back into place, do not wiggle your butt, smooth your dress and sit down

A pretty sitting posture is when you keep your knees together and ankles together, sit tall with your hands in your lap

You can also cross your legs above the knees, hold legs close together.

Walk gracefully, hold your head high, remain straight from the hips up, walk smoothly and keep your steps moderate

Point your feet in a straight line, do not move your hips unnecessarily

Standing like a lady, stand tall with feet 2 inches apart place the toe of the right foot with the left arch.

Body Image

Body image is how you see yourself when you look in the mirror or when you picture yourself in your mind.

You can study your body image in a mirror this helps you maintain a positive body image or improve your body image.

Body image and positive self-esteem are closely related.

Appearance is not the only way to maintain a positive body image. You need a positive attitude toward food and exercise.

Positive body image is keeping your body clean by bathing daily, wearing clean clothes, clean underwear, and deodorant and body lotion to keep your skin soft and moisturized.

Personal appearance is important your clothes should be neat and clean and fit properly.

Wear clothing that is comfortable and make you feel good about your body.

When you look good you feel good about yourself. Looking good and feeling good can promote positive self-esteem.

Keep a journal of the things you like and dislike about your body image and began to improve your image if needed.

Your Personal Appearance

Your personal appearance is very important you are judged by how you look. I am not saying it is right but this is the way our society is.

Keep your hair neat and clean in a style that flatters your face. If you wear makeup make sure it is age appropriate and not too heavy. Keep your skin clean and fresh.

Wear moderate size jewelry, no tattoos, no face piercing, no nose rings, and no tongue rings, these things take away from your personal appearance and could interfere with you getting a job.

Make sure your clothes fit properly, not to tight or short.

Make sure your buttons are intact on your clothes and that there are no tears or rips on your clothes.

Makes sure your hemline is intact. Make sure your clothes are clean and pressed.

Always look in the mirror before leaving home to make sure you are looking your best.

Dressing For All Ocassions

It is important know how to dress for all occasion.

CAUSAL WEAR can be clothes that you wear to school, slacks, skirts, dresses, jumpers, blouse, causal shoes or boots. You will wear causal wear to the movie, school, to the mall, out to dinner with friends of visit friends and family.

PLAY WEAR–shorts, jogging clothes, jeans, exercise wear, swim wear, you can wear tennis shoes, sandals, these clothe can be worn on the play, beach, tennis court and the gymnasium.

SEMI-FORMAL can be a fancy dress, dress shoe, stockings, earring and necklace, you would dress like this for church social, school dance or a dressy family affair.

FORMAL WEAR can; be a long gown, dress shoes, stocking and nice jewelry, this type of dress is good for a prom, military ball.

Always dress so that you will be comfortable and look in style.

Personal Hygiene

Person hygiene is keeping your body clean. Bathing every day is important, keeping your body clean can prevent odors and germs, use your favorite soap, a clean wash cloth and towel. Always use your deodorant under arm to prevent odor. You must change your bra and panties each day because your undergarments can hold odor.

Keep your hands clean, nails clean filed and trimmed. Do not wear chipped finger nail polish, it shows that you are not taking of care of your nails.

Keep your feet clean and dry too prevent odors and skin irritations. Keep your toe nails trimmed.

Change socks or stockings daily, keep the inside of your shoes dry and clean and wash your tennis shoes to prevent odor. Your friends will enjoy being around you when you have a clean and fresh smelling body free from odor.

Prevent bad breath by brushing your teeth 3 times a day and keeping your regular dental appointments. Some foods can cause bad breath. We are told that we need to brush our teeth in the morning, before bed and after each meal, sometimes we are in school or out eating in a public place and we just can't brush. It would be great to brush in the morning and before bed time, and any time after meal if you are at home.

Making A Good First Impression

You only get one chance to make a good first impression. When you meet a person for the first time, give a greeting and a smile. Your greeting can be pleasant like how are you? I am pleased to meet you, make eye contact. You may extent your right hand for a handshake.

Body language speaks louder than words. In psychology a first impression is the event when one person first encounters another person and forms a mental image of that person. It can take 7 seconds to make an impression.

You are judged by way you dress, sit, stand and walk. You are judged by the way you speak and interact with others.

In seconds after meeting you, people will get an opinion of who they think you are.

Remember you only get one chance to make a good first impression and a first impression is a lasting impression.

Health Awarness

It is very good to be aware of signs and symptoms of illness and changes in your body and your health. If there is something that you are concerned about talk it over with your parents or the school nurse for starts then your parent will take you to your Doctor for an examination and test.

When a person has good health they can function well physically, mentally, socially and spiritually and reach their full body potentials.

To help make sure you maintain good health you need to eat proper nutrition such as vegetables, proteins foods that give you the vitamin and minerals that you need.

Drink water every day and get your proper rest and exercise. Keep your body clean.

Physical Exercise

It is important to do physical activity every day.

Exercise is movement of the body using muscles and flexibility movement of the bone it will improve the flexibility of the body movement. Exercise can help you keep your weight down, make you feel better and cause relaxation after exercise.

There are many ways to exercise by walking, dancing, jumping rope, hula hooping, jogging, running, playing tennis, aerobic and swimming.

If you can join an organized sport in school or community center, boys and girls club and YMCA will have programs that you can get exercise.

Obesity

Obesity is a condition of excessive amount of accumulation and the storage of fat in the body causing one to be overweight or obese.

Being overweight or obese can cause low self-esteem and unhealthy body image. If you are dealing with obesity there is help. You can go to your Doctor and get information on weight loss and proper eating habits he can also have you to see a nutritionist.

Getting started on your goal set to lose weight, keep a journal

Write down what you eat in a day. Then you can write down the calories that you are taking in. You can plan a menu for breakfast, lunch and dinner. There are healthy snacks, like fruits, carrots sticks and celery. It is good to drink at least 8 glasses of water day.

Exercise is also very good to help with decreasing obesity.

Walking, swimming and aerobics are some good exercises to start with.

There is a problem of obesity among adolescent girls. Some of the problems obesity can cause are:

1. Low self-esteem

2. Unhealthy body image.

3. Health problems and illness.

4. Unable to wear the clothes you want to wear because they will not fit properly.

5. You cannot move around as easily as desired.

6. Poor social interactions with peer.

7. Dating can be difficult.

8. Travel, it is difficult to sit in the seats on the bus, airplane, train and the movie seats.

Healthy Eating Habits

The word nutrition means what is in our food and how it is used

In side of us. Everything we eat is made up of a variety of chemicals; those our bodies use are called nutrients.

Beans, grain and dried fruit are rich source of the nutrients our body need. Foods give us energy.

Your body needs these six kinds of nutrients to stay healthy.

1. Carbohydrates-energy uses to fuel the brain and muscles. Consist of starches and dietary fiber.

2. Protein-used in building and repair muscles, red blood cells, hair and other tissues and making hormones.

3. Fat —— maintain skin and hair, cushion our vital organs, provide insulation and is necessary for the production and absorption of certain vitamins and hormone.

4. Vitamin —— help to regulate chemical reaction in the body, you get vitamin through a varied diet. Basically from the food you eat.

5. Mineral —— help many body functions, bone structure, red blood cells and transport oxygen to red blood cells, hair, skin, and teeth, nerve functions, muscles and metabolic process such as those that turn the food we eat into energy.

6. Water —— is a vital nutrient for good health most of our body weight 60-70% is made up of water. Water help control our body temperature, carries nutrients and waste products from our cells needed for cell function it is recommended to drink at least 8 glasses of water a day.

Bernetta Watson

More healthy eating habits

Say no to sugary candy they have no nutritional value except for calories in the sugar.

Say no to sodas and unhealthy snacks like chips, candy, cookie these have no nutritional value, they taste good if you must eat them, eat them in moderation.

Leadership

A leader can organize and lead a group of people. A leader leads by example. A good leader can get the job done and delegate responsibilities to the organization or the group effectively.

To be a leader you must have positive self-esteem, good social skills, effect communication skills, good life skills.

Personal appearance you must be neat and clean, good manners and a positive attitude.

A good leader has good civility skills, is always kind and polite to people. To be a good leader you must know how to treat others in a kind and respectful way. Make others feels good about them self.

People will know if you are a good leader. Do you want to be a good leader? You know what you need to do is lead by example.

Poem
Be A Good Leader

I want every little girl of color who's told she is "Bossy" to be told she has leadership skills.

A leader can work well others.

A leader has the ability to work toward a common goal.

A leader is honest, flexible and has good manners.

A leader has good social skills.

A leader is well groomed, impeccable personal hygiene and personal appearance.

LEAD BY EXAMPLE

By Bernetta Watson

Peer Pressure

A peer is a person who is the equal to another in abilities, qualification, age, background and status. Your girl friends are your peers. They can cause you peer pressure by harassing you and attempting to pressure you with social issues, like you should wear makeup and you don't want to wear makeup.

They will try to tell you how to dress. Telling you need a boyfriend to be up with the times this is peer pressure that is not acceptable because you do not want a boyfriend at this time.

There is some good peer pressure when your friends challenge you to keep your grades up in school or when you have friends that encourage you to do the right things. Like your homework, study time or to use good manners.

Bulling

A bully is a person that torment, intimidate, harass, is mean, terrorize smaller or weaker persons. The bully 'reason to act like this is because she or he wants to think they can get away with it, don't let them, we must stop the bully.

When a person is bulling you, making you feel uncomfortable or afraid. Let everyone know about what is happening to you, your teacher if is at school. Your parents need to talk to the bully's parents.

You need help to stop the bully you can't do it alone. Most important the bully parents need to know if his or her child's behavior continues then the police must be called because bulling is a serious problem. No one deserves to be bullied.

A BULLY CAN MAKE YOUR LIFE VERY UNCOMFOTABLE IT MUST STOP.

Say No To Bullying

Be self-confident

Be brave

Be caring about your feelings

Be proud of yourself

Be sure that you do not have to except bulling, tell someone that can and will help you, stop the bully.

Say no to being bullied.

Be sure to know you will grow up to be a beautiful person, successful and accomplished.

Be sure that the bully will be bulling people and be sad and alone.

POEM by Bernetta Watson

QUOTE: "you may not control all events that happen to you but you can decide not to be reduced by them."

Maya Angelo

Setting Goals

Setting goals will help you achieve your dreams. One of the goals you should be working toward is a good education and good grades in school. Only you can make this happen by studying hard, do your homework on time, and do all your special assignments and projects. If you need help tell your teacher and parents so you can get help, or a tutor will help or a study group.

Good grades can help you get into college with the possibility of receiving a scholarship.

A good education can get you ready for a good future in your employment. A good education can give you a good salary and help you live a comfortable life style.

Always Set Goals

A goal is a point, end or place one is striving to reach.

Always set goals.

Goals are dreams.

Goals give you something to look and work toward.

Set goals for school and making good grades.

Set a goal to get a summer job when you are old enough.

Set a goal to save your money, open a bank account.

Set a goal to graduate from high school and attend college and graduate.

Set a goal to get training in a career or profession that you will enjoy doing.

Always set goals.

Poem by Bernetta Watson

Designing A Vision Board

A vision board is a powerful tool to help you visualize your future plans and goals. A vision board is a dream board.

Vision board can be motivation toward your goals.

These are the instructions on how to prepare a vision board. And the items needed to prepare the vision board.

1. Glue

2. Scissors

3. Pencils

4. Crayon

5. Poster board size 18x22, white in color

6. Old magazines, newspapers, all these items can be purchased from the dollar store. If you do not have them at home.

   Decide what your goals are for the future.
   Example: if you plan to go to college cut out a picture of a college, the type of house you plan to live, do you want to be in the military?, do plan to play sports, what type of clothes, shoes do you want wear, what is your favorite pet? Type of car you want, food you like to eat. Do you like boats, race cars, and airplane?
   CUT THESE THINGS OUT OF THE MAGAZINE OR NEWS PAPER OR YOU CAN DRAW ON YOUR VISION BOARD.

   You will make a collage of the pictures, these are your goal put on the vision board you can keep your vision board to keep your goals insight, share your vision board with your family and friends.
   A vision board is motivation toward your future goals.

Hand Washing

It is very important that you wash your hands before sitting down to eat a meal or before setting the table.

You have many germs on your hands that you can't see with the human eye that can make you sick if you don't wash your hands before touching food that will be going into your mouth and into your stomachs.

The proper way to wash your hands is to turn on the water, then apply soap to your hands, rub liquid soap between your fingers and hands under the running water for at least 20 seconds, use a paper to dry your hands after drying your hands put that towel in the trash then use a clean paper towel to turn off the running water.

Table Manners

One important social skill for children and teens is knowing proper table manners. Meals are social events, it is important to use proper manners at home, school, restaurants, while visiting friends and family.

This includes setting the table. Table manners rules are not complicated, but will help you make a great impression at meal time. When you have good table manners family and friends will enjoy eating with you.

Table Manners

Learning table manners can be fun, and you will use them all your life. The first thing we will learn is how to set the table properly.

The way the forks, knives, spoons, glasses, cups, plates, bowls and napkins are arranged on the tablecloth or placemat is called a "place setting".

A Basic Place Setting

This is the correct way to place your plate and eating utensils when you do a place setting.

Drinking glass

Left   PLATE   right

Napkin-fork   knife-spoon

Always wash your hands before sitting down for a meal.

The napkin is the most important part of the place setting.

The napkin is on the left side of the plate.

You can also see your napkin placed in the center of the plate it will be folded.

If you leave the table places your napkin in your chair.

When you have finished your meal, place your napkin on the left side of your plate.

How to use your napkin

Take your napkin off the table, unfold the napkin, and place in your lap as soon as you sit down.

Always use your napkin to dab your mouth for any excess food, always use your napkin before taking sip of liquids.

Learning The Cloth Napkin Rules

Place the napkin in your lap with folded edge toward the knees. When you lift the napkin by the folded edge and use it to wipe your mouth, you will not get any food stains on your clothes when you replace it in your lap.

Use it to dab your mouth

Dab your mouth with it before drinking from a glass so smudges will not be on the glass.

Leave the napkin in your lap until you get up to leave the table. When you are temporarily away from and when you leave for the last time, place the used napkin to the left of your plate. Never refold a napkin.

Never put a napkin on a plate.

Dining Conversation

Make sure your conversation is pleasant you don't want to spoil some ones appetite by saying words that are inappropriate or gross. Think, listen and look before you start a conversation.

Talk about light issues like the weather, your flower garden or a vacation.

When you have a need to go to the ladies room just excuse yourself, please don't make an announcement about what you are going to the bathroom for.

Table Manners Don'ts

1. No elbows on table

2. Do not talk with food in your mouth. No one wants to see food in your mouth while they are eating.

3. Do not talk about things that will gross people out like (a dead fog you cut up in biology class.)

4. If you need to be excused to go to the bathroom. Do not make an announcement I am going to the bathroom just say excuse me, place your napkin on the chair. Please wash your hand after bath room use.

5. If you cough or sneeze excuse yourself from the table until it is under control. Wash your hands before you return to the table.

6. No loud talking or laughing during the meal.

7. No putting on lipstick while setting at the dinner table.

8. No combing your hair while at the dinner table.

9. If you use and have good table manners your friends will enjoy going out with you for meals or inviting you to their homes.

Table Manners Do's

TABLE MANNERS DO'S

1. Always wash your hands before eating your meal.

2. Use your napkin (cloth) napkin, when you sit down open your napkin, off the table place it in your lap.

3. Waite until the grace is said before you start to eat. The guest of honor or the host or hostess will tell you when to begin eating.

4. If you are asked for the salt, pass both the salt and pepper that is the correct thing to do.

5. Never reach across the table for food ask someone to pass the food to you.

6. If you would like to share a food items with a person eating with you do not eat off a person, plate ask for a small plate and get a sample of the food put on the small plate.

7. Use your indoor voice and talk about pleasant things.

8. When drinking your water or other liquids at the dinner table take small sips not gulps of your liquids.

9. When cutting up your meat only cut one piece at a time.

10. Proper way to butter your bread is to break off a piece of bread, butter that piece of bread eat that, never butter your entire piece of bread.

11. Once you use your eating utensil do not place them on the table.

Posture And Behavior At The Dining Table

When you are eating a meal sit up straight and keep your feet flat on the floor, no kicking the person sitting across from you.

Keep your elbows off the table. When you need something that is on the table, like a food item, salt or pepper don't reach across the table ask the person sitting next to you to pass the item that you need. Remember say to please and thank you.

When you are dining remember to use your indoor voice, no loud talking and laughing it is rude and there is risk when talking with food in your mouth you could choke.

Avoid having conversation at the dining table that is unpleasant and might gross a person out. You should not talk about a person vomiting, or seeing a dead animal or using the bathroom. Don't talk about your illness or someone else illness, talk about pleasant, think, listen before you start a conversation.

HOW TO BUTTER YOUR BREAD

First you break off a small piece of bread, butter that piece eat it then break of the next piece when you are ready to eat it. Never butter all your bread at the same time.

HOW TO CUT YOUR MEAT UP.

When cutting your meat only cut one piece at a time, eat that piece then cut the next piece eat it, never cut all your meat at one time.

FOODS THAT CAN BE EATEN WITH YOUR FINGERS.

1. Pizza

2. Chicken wing, chicken legs.

3. Sandwiches

4. Hot dogs

5. Hamburgers

6. Fruit

7. Chips

8. Cookies

9. Bread

10. Candy or many other snacks.

ALLERGY

Make sure you do not have allergies to foods that you eat your mother, father and the Doctor will know if you have allergy and will explain which food you should not eat.

FOODS THAT ARE DIFFICULT TO EAT.

Peas-to be eaten with fork.

Lobster- to be eaten with your hands and knife and fork.

Spaghetti - to be eaten with knife and fork.

Crabs- with hand and fingers.

Asparagus-with finger and knife and fork.

EATING SOUP

Soup should always be eaten with a spoon.

Eating Soup

Never blow into your soup, never leave your spoon in your soup bowl it could tip over spill soup on the person next to you.

Never season your soup before you taste it.

Do not slurp your soup.

Eat your soup with a spoon hold the spoon at the end of the handle on your middle finger, with your thumb on top.

Dip the spoon sideways into the soup, then skim from the front of the bowl to the back. Sip from the side of the spoon.

Soup is usually served in a bowl with a dish or a charger under the bowl you can place your spoon on the edge of the plate don't leave the spoon in the bowl.

If you have soup left in the bottom of the bowl do not drink your soup from the bowl.

The salt and pepper shaker rule

When having a meal and a person ask you to please pass the salt.

The rule of passing the salt and pepper is passing both of them at the same time.

Drinking Liquids

You will be drinking liquids with your meal; please so not slurp your water, soda, milk, juice or tea. Take small sips.

When you sit down for a meal your beverage glass will always be on your right side of your plate at the tip of the knife.

Before drinking from your glass always use your napkin to dab your mouth to keep food products and lipstick from the rim of your glass.

Poems By Bernetta

QUOTES BY POSITIVE AFRICAN AMERICAN WOMEN

POEMS

Forgiveness

Smile

The color yellow

A good deed

Girl's behavior in public places

The Arts

Poem

FORGIVENESS

When someone does something you do not like and it hurts you.

Do not hold a grudge you can forgive but do not forget.

The forgiving is for you to help you feel better.

The person may never say I AM SORRY.

BY Bernetta Watson

QUOTE: BY MAYA ANGELO

"It's one of the greatest gift you can give yourself is to forgive, forgive everybody" Maya Angelo

Poem

SMILE

When you smile you make people happy and they will return the smile.

A smile can brighten a person's day.

SO SMILE, SMILE, SMILE, SMILE, SMILE.

By Bernetta Watson

Quote: by a famous writer

"If you have only one smile in you give it to the people you love"

Maya Angelo

The Color Yellow

Yellow is bright like the sun

Yellow is a happy color

Yellow is a confident color

When I wear the color yellow it brightens my day and makes me feel happy.

Poem by Bernetta Watson

Quote: "The color yellow is associated with creativity, clear thoughts, self-confidence and optimism."

From the book title Project Butterfly

Author Neambi Jaha

A Good Deed

Always try to do a good deed every day.

Do something that is easy, helpful and kind.

Speak to a teacher or friend at school with a smile and a good morning greeting.

Help your teacher clean up a mess in the classroom.

Help your mother with chores around your home.

Help your younger sisters and brothers with their homework.

Good deeds are always appreciated and they will make you feel good, when you help someone else.

Poem by Bernetta

Girls Behavior In Public Places

Be an example for other girls.

Be polite.

Be well mannered.

No loud talking, use your indoor voice.

When eating out always use good table manners.

Always be well groomed.

Always remember your behavior in public places; someone is always observing your behavior.

Poem by Bernetta Watson

The Arts

Art is a diverse range of human activities in creating visual auditory or performing artworks, expressing imaginative or technical skills, intended to be appreciated for their beauty or emotional power. It is human behavior.

Always participate in the arts. The arts of your choice can help you define who you are and strengthen you.

DANCING	THEATER	DRAMA	POETRY
PLAYS	SINGING	MUSIC	FASHION DESIGN
		MUSEUMS	
THE ART OF GOOD MANNERS	ART	PAINTING	WRITING

QUOTE: Michelle Obama

"The arts are not just a nice thing to have or to do if there is free time or if you can afford it. Rather, painting and poetry, music and fashion design and dialogue, they define who we are as a people and provide an account of our history, for the next generation." "Michelle Obama"

Printed in the United States
By Bookmasters